Editor
Eric Migliaccio

Managing Editor
Ina Massler Levin, M.A.

Editor-in-Chief
Sharon Coan, M.S. Ed.

Cover Artist
Barb Lorseyedi

Art Manager
Kevin Barnes

Imaging
Craig Gunnell

Product Manager
Phil Garcia

Publisher
Mary D. Smith, M.S. Ed.

Practice Makes Perfect

Main Idea

GRADE 3

Includes practice for Standardized Tests

Teacher Created Resources

TCR 8643

D1476100

Author

Debra J. Housel, M.S. Ed.

Teacher Created Resources, Inc.
12621 Western Avenue
Garden Grove, CA 92841
www.teachercreated.com
ISBN: 978-0-7439-8643-4

©2004 Teacher Created Resources, Inc.
Reprinted, 2019
Made in U.S.A.

Table of Contents

Introduction

The old adage "practice makes perfect" can apply to your child and his or her education. The more practice and exposure your child has with concepts being taught in school, the more success he or she is likely to find. For many parents, knowing how to help their children may be frustrating because the resources may not be readily available. As a parent, it is also hard to know where to focus your efforts so that the extra practice your child receives at home supports what he or she is learning in school.

A child's ability to understand what he or she reads depends largely upon the ability to locate the main idea of a passage and identify the details that support it. *Practice Makes Perfect: Main Idea* covers identifying the main idea and supporting details in both fiction and nonfiction text. To allow for the greatest variety of practice, the passages are not complete stories. The exercises included in this book meet or reinforce educational standards and objectives similar to the ones required by your state and school district for third-graders:

☞ The student will identify the main idea in fiction and nonfiction text.

☞ The student will locate supporting details in fiction and nonfiction text.

☞ The student will identify topic sentences in paragraphs.

☞ The student will choose the best title for a passage.

Introduction (cont.)

How to Make the Most of This Book

☞ Set aside a specific place in your home to work on this book. Keep the necessary materials on hand.

☞ Determine a specific time of day to work on these practice pages to establish consistency. Look for times in your day or week that are conducive to practicing skills.

☞ Keep all practice sessions with your child positive and constructive. If your child becomes frustrated or tense, set aside the book and look for another time to practice. Do not force your child to perform or use this book as a punishment.

☞ Allow the child to use whatever writing instrument he or she prefers.

☞ Review and praise the work your child has done.

Things to Remember About the Main Idea in Nonfiction

Make certain that your child understands the way that authors typically present ideas in nonfiction materials. Nonfiction writers use different paragraph structures. In the following examples, the main idea is italicized:

Paragraph Structure #1

The main idea is directly stated as the first sentence of a paragraph. The rest of the paragraph provides the supporting details:

> *Clara Barton, known as America's first nurse, was a brave and devoted humanitarian.* While caring for others, she was shot at, got frostbitten fingers, had severe laryngitis twice, burned her hands, and almost lost her eyesight. Yet she continued to care for the sick and injured until she died at the age of 91.

Paragraph Structure #2

The main idea may be in the center of the paragraph, surrounded on both sides by details:

> The coral have created a reef where more than 200 kinds of birds and about 1,500 types of fish live. *In fact, Australia's Great Barrier Reef provides a home for a great variety of interesting animals.* These include sea turtles, giant clams, crabs, and crown-of-thorns starfish.

Paragraph Structure #3

The main idea comes at the end of the paragraph as a summary of the details that came before:

> Each year Antarctica spends six months in darkness, from mid March to mid September. The continent is covered year-round by ice, which causes sunlight to reflect off its surface. It never really warms up. The coldest temperature ever recorded on Earth was in Antarctica. *Antarctica has one of the harshest environments in the world.*

Introduction *(cont.)*

Things to Remember About the Main Idea in Nonfiction

Paragraph Structure #4

The main idea is not directly stated and must be inferred from the details given in the paragraph. This paragraph structure is the most challenging and the least common in nonfiction text for children:

> The biggest sea horse ever found was over a foot long. Large sea horses live along the coasts of New Zealand, Australia, and California. Smaller sea horses live off the coast of Florida, in the Caribbean Sea, and in the Gulf of Mexico. The smallest adult sea horse ever found was only one half-inch long!

In this example, the implied main idea is that sea horses' sizes vary based on where they live. When the main idea isn't stated, the student must pull together the details to ascertain the key idea. A good way to do this is to think about the "reporter questions": who, did what, when, where, and why. The passage may present the answers in any order.

Things to Remember About the Main Idea in Fiction

☞ Unlike nonfiction text, literature rarely has paragraphs with topic sentences and supporting details. Often in fictional text, the main idea is never directly stated anywhere in the passage. This can present a challenging task for your young student. One of the best ways for a student to ascertain the main idea in fiction is to "form a movie" in his or her mind. This changing visualization will help the child to figure out the key idea.

☞ Just as they do in nonfiction, the answers to the questions <u>who</u>, <u>did, what</u>, <u>when</u>, <u>where</u>, <u>why</u>, and <u>how</u> lead a reader to the details in fiction. A compilation of the details can also be helpful in identifying the main idea. Even so, without a topic sentence, stating the main idea requires paraphrasing, which is a higher-level thinking skill.

☞ In literature, the main idea is often embedded in emotions—the emotions of the characters and the emotions of the reader. Well-written fiction makes the reader feel as if he or she is "there" and actually experiencing the events in the story. Therefore, encourage your student to notice the emotions of the character. Ask leading questions such as, "How would you feel if you were [character's name]? Why? Do you think [character's name] feels like you do? Why?"

The main idea is what a passage is about as a whole. Forming pictures as you read helps you focus on the main idea. Make a "movie in your mind."

Passage 1

Haley was so excited that she practically danced into the pet shop. She was about to meet her first pet! Her mother had promised her that she could choose a small animal. Haley looked at bunnies, hamsters, rats, and mice. There were so many to choose from! She wondered how she could decide.

Then, in the corner cage, she saw the cutest animal she'd ever seen. With its black and white bands of fur, it looked like a tiny panda bear. Haley knew that she wanted that guinea pig.

What is the main idea?

ⓐ Haley can't decide which guinea pig she wants as a pet.

ⓑ Haley can't decide what kind of animal she'd like as a pet.

● Haley chooses a guinea pig for her first pet.

Which sentences in the passage helped you to figure out the main idea?

ⓐ Haley was so excited that she practically danced into the pet shop. AND Her mother had promised her that she could choose a small animal.

ⓑ Haley looked at bunnies, hamsters, rats, and mice. AND She wondered how she could decide.

● She was about to meet her first pet! AND Haley knew that she wanted that guinea pig.

Passage 2

James Merlin made the first pair of in-line skates in 1760. His skates had wooden spools in a row. He wore them to a party and ran into a mirror. He never wore them again. Few people tried skating, but those that did copied Merlin's skate design. In 1863 James Plimpton decided to change the design. He made skates with four spread-out wheels. This style was the only kind of wheeled skate for over 100 years.

Then in 1980 Scott Olsen saw a pair of old in-line skates. He played hockey and wanted to keep his skills strong year round. He knew other hockey players and ice skaters wanted to train without ice, too. They needed skates that moved like ice skates. Olsen made a new pair of in-line skates. He called them Rollerblades.

People got excited when they saw the new skates. Even those who didn't ice skate wanted to try them. Once they did, they lost interest in roller skates. Now many people like in-line skating better than any other kind of skating.

What is the main idea?

ⓐ In-line skates were popular during the 1700s.

ⓑ In-line skates have replaced roller skates in popularity.

ⓒ Hockey players and ice skaters are the only people who use in-line skates.

Which sentences in the passage helped you to figure out the main idea?

ⓐ He knew other hockey players and ice skaters wanted to train without ice, too. They needed skates that moved like ice skates.

ⓑ James Merlin made the first pair of in-line skates in 1760. His skates had wooden spools in a row.

ⓒ People got excited when they saw the new skates. AND Once they did, they lost interest in rollerskates. Now many people like in-line skating better than any other kind of skating.

Passage 3

Suddenly Lori had an idea. "Suppose these boxes were piled here to hide a door," she cried.

"Why would you think that?" Brad asked.

"Because we know that the men came in here. They aren't in here. If the way we came in is the only way out, they'd have had to walk right past us," Lori reasoned.

"Which they didn't," Caleb pointed out. "That means that there has to be another way out of here."

Caleb and Lori began moving the cardboard boxes as quickly as they could.

Brad protested, "If the men went through a door behind those boxes, how did the boxes get back in front of the door?" He crossed his arms and rolled his eyes toward the ceiling. His jaw dropped.

"Caleb! Lori! Stop moving those boxes and look what I've found!" Brad said excitedly.

What is the main idea?

ⓐ Caleb, Lori, and Brad move boxes to look for a hidden door.

ⓑ Caleb, Lori, and Brad find the men hiding behind a secret door.

ⓒ While Caleb and Lori move boxes, Brad finds something exciting.

Which sentence(s) in the passage helped you to figure out the main idea?

ⓐ "Because we know that the men came in here. They aren't in here. If the way we came in is the only way out, they'd have had to walk right past us," Lori reasoned.

ⓑ Caleb and Lori began moving cardboard boxes as quickly as they could. AND "Caleb! Lori! Stop moving those boxes and look what I've found!" Brad said excitedly.

ⓒ Brad protested, "If the men went through a door behind those boxes, how did the boxes get back in front of the door?"

Passage 4

Easter Island lies in the South Pacific Ocean. Although it is not large, many people know its name. Easter Island is famous because of its giant statues. These statues look like people. They are hundreds of years old. Those who lived on the island long ago made them. They probably did it to honor dead relatives.

Even with the modern tools of today, it would be hard to create such statues. Yet these were carved by hand. Large, red rocks sit atop the heads of some of the statues. Balancing those stones must have been very difficult.

What is the main idea?

ⓐ Easter Island has large statues that were hard to build.

ⓑ People with modern tools have fixed the giant statues on Easter Island.

ⓒ The giant statues on Easter Island were famous at one time.

Which sentences in the passage helped you to figure out the main idea?

ⓐ Large, red rocks sit atop the heads of some of the statues. AND Balancing those stones must have been very difficult.

ⓑ Easter Island is famous because of its giant statues. AND Even with the modern tools of today, it would be hard to create such statues.

ⓒ Easter Island lies in the South Pacific Ocean. AND Although it is not large, many people know its name. Easter Island is famous because of its giant statues.

Passage 5

Fred waded into the rice paddy, frowning as the muddy water filled his shoes. He reached the first field worker and asked in his best Chinese, "Did you see a light blue pickup truck drive by here?"

The woman looked bewildered, so Fred repeated his question. She turned and shouted to the others, "This man wants to know if we've seen a light blue pickup truck go by."

The other three women, young and old, stopped their work. They spoke quietly among themselves.

Fred felt annoyed. Whoever had taken his truck could be halfway to Beijing by now! All he wanted was a simple "yes" or "no."

"Please—I need to know right now. My truck was stolen. I must find it!"

The oldest woman in the group stepped forward. "Was it brand new and very shiny?" she asked.

Fred shook his head impatiently. "No it wasn't. In fact it was covered with mud. Did you see my truck or not?"

What is the main idea?

ⓐ Fred gets frustrated trying to find out if the workers have seen his stolen truck.

ⓑ Fred finds his stolen pickup truck in a rice paddy.

ⓒ The oldest woman in the group has seen Fred's truck recently.

Which sentences in the passage helped you to figure out the main idea?

ⓐ Fred waded into the rice paddy. He reached the first field worker and asked in his best Chinese, "Did you see a light blue pickup truck drive by here?"

ⓑ The oldest woman in the group stepped forward. "Was it brand new and very shiny?" she asked.

ⓒ Fred felt annoyed. Whoever had taken his truck could be halfway to Beijing by now! AND Fred shook his head impatiently. "Did you see my truck or not?"

Passage 6

Most people write with their right hand. Some people use their left hand to write. Most likely, no one taught you which hand to use. You were born right-handed or left-handed. More than one out of every ten people is left-handed. They use their left hand when they open a door, eat with utensils, and move a computer mouse.

Many things, like scissors and can openers, are made for the 87 percent of people that use their right hands. Lefties usually learn how to use such tools easily. In the past, people thought that left-handed people needed to change. They wanted lefties to switch to using their right hands. Teachers made students write with their right hands, even if that felt strange to them. Some lefties did change hands. A few became ambidextrous. That meant they could use both of their hands equally well.

What is the main idea?

ⓐ Most left-handed people use both of their hands equally well.

ⓑ People who are left-handed struggle to use scissors and can openers.

ⓒ Although a person is born left-handed, people used to try to make them change.

Which sentence(s) in the passage helped you to figure out the main idea?

ⓐ Many things, like scissors and can openers, are made for the 87 percent of people that use their right hands.

ⓑ You were born right handed or left-handed. AND In the past, people thought that left-handed people needed to change.

ⓒ Some lefties became ambidextrous. That meant they could use both of their hands equally well.

You can find the main idea by looking for the answers to these questions:

☞ **Who/What?**   ☞ **When?**   ☞ **Why?**

☞ **Did What?**   ☞ **Where?**

Passage 1

The deep shadows of the forest seemed to press closer, as if wrapping Eve in a cloak. She wished she could get a fire started. Something had gone wrong with each match she had lit. Her shaking hands had dropped the first one. The second fizzled out on leaves that weren't dry enough to catch fire. The third she'd held to the kindling until it burned her fingertips. Eve only had one more match. If she failed to get a fire going with this one, she'd spend the night in this heavy darkness.

Find the answers to these questions.

Who/What?: _____

Did What?: _____

When?: _____at night_____

Where?:_____

Why?: _____

What is the main idea?

ⓐ Eve is thrilled when she manages to light a fire on her fourth try.

ⓑ Eve has a hard time trying to start a fire.

ⓒ Eve is wrapped in a heavy cloak because she can't get a fire started, and the forest is cold.

Passage 2

Amelia Earhart was a U.S. pilot. She was the first woman to fly alone across the Atlantic Ocean. That trip made her famous. But a mystery surrounds her last flight. She and her navigator, Fred Noonan, vanished. No trace has ever been found of them. No one has ever found any pieces of their plane. Many people have searched over the years.

In May 1937 the pair took off on a flight. They planned to fly around the world. Earhart would be the first woman to do so. Newspapers and the U.S. Navy kept track of their trip. Things seemed fine until July 2. Then she radioed a ship that she was almost out of gas. What happened next is unclear. People on several islands said that they saw a plane crash into the Pacific Ocean. Others said they saw the pair as prisoners on a Japanese-held island. Some believe that the Japanese thought they were spies and killed them. We may never know for sure.

Find the answers to these questions.

Who/What?: _____

Did What?: __vanished_____

When?: _____

Where?:_____

Why?: _____

What is the main idea?

ⓐ A mystery surrounds Amelia Earhart's last flight.

ⓑ Over the years many people have searched for the pair.

ⓒ Amelia Earhart and Fred Noonan crashed their plane into the Pacific Ocean.

Passage 3

"Let's go home," George said to Ralph.

"But I haven't bought anything yet," Ralph protested.

"Well hurry up! I want to go home and play checkers."

Ralph looked at many different things while George stood, impatiently tapping his foot.

Finally, Ralph sighed. "George, I can't find anything."

"OK, fine, then let's go."

"I really want to get something," Ralph insisted.

"Then how about this set of dominoes?" George asked.

"I don't have nearly enough money for that," Ralph replied.

George raised an eyebrow. "Just how much money do you have, Ralph?"

"A dime," replied Ralph.

George burst out, "You dragged me to this garage sale when all you have to spend is 10 cents?"

Find the answers to these questions.

Who/What?: _____

Did What?: _got annoyed at Ralph_____

When?: _____

Where?:_____

Why?: _____

What is the main idea?

ⓐ George gets upset at Ralph when Ralph won't lend him a dime.

ⓑ George is eager to go home and play checkers.

ⓒ George gets upset when he finds that Ralph has made him go to a garage sale when he only has a dime.

Passage 4

Just then the boys heard the sound of keys jingling as someone approached the door of the room. They looked wildly at each other, certain that any second they'd hear the sound of the key in the lock.

"Hide!" Dan whispered, urgently pointing toward the crates.

The boys hurried behind the boxes stacked in one corner of the room. Over the top of the crates someone had thrown a Persian rug. It draped down over both edges of the stack. With any luck, it would help to conceal them completely. No sooner had they hidden themselves than they heard the door open. They froze in position, determined not to move a muscle. Ron fought the urge to sneeze.

A light switch clicked on and light filled the room. Footsteps came toward the crates. Both boys held their breath. Had the person heard them in their haste to hide?

Find the answers to these questions.

Who/What?: _____

Did What?: _____

When?: _____they heard someone coming_____

Where?:_____

Why?: _____

What is the main idea?

ⓐ Dan and Ron are terrified that their hiding place will be found.

ⓑ The person who enters the room discovers Dan and Ron.

ⓒ Dan and Ron hide a friend behind some crates.

Passage 5

In August 1995 Joe Terry, then 15, received the Carnegie Medal for Bravery. He had saved two little children. It happened on some railroad tracks in California. Josh Gallegos, 3, and his sister, Jenny, 1, had left their yard. They wandered away and started to play on the railroad tracks. Their mother did not know where they went. As a train roared toward them at 60 miles an hour, Jenny sat on a rail. Josh stood between the rails. He bent down to pick up rocks.

Joe Terry was sitting on his front porch. He heard the train coming. He looked across the road and saw the tiny children on the tracks. He had no time to call for help. Joe ran across four lanes of traffic. Although a car nearly hit the teen, he never slowed down. When he reached the children, Joe pushed Josh out of the way and grabbed Jenny. Holding her, he jumped. Although the train knocked the baseball cap off Joe's head, no one got injured.

Find the answers to these questions.

Who/What?: _____

Did What?: ___rescued two little children_____

When?: _____

Where?:_____

Why?: _____

What is the main idea?

Ⓒ Joe Terry acted on his own because he had no time to call for help.

Ⓑ Joe Terry saved two kids from being hit by a train.

Ⓒ The Gallegos children had wandered away from their home.

Passage 6

The noise seemed to come from behind the Dumpster. Dana crept closer. The overwhelming smell of rotting trash made her turn away. Then she heard it again. It sounded just like a baby crying. Nobody would leave a baby behind a Dumpster, would they? Holding her nose with her fingers, she approached the smelly Dumpster.

Dana glanced around. There was nobody else in the alley. She wondered if she could move the heavy Dumpster by herself. First, she tugged and pulled. Then she pushed and shoved. All she managed to do was move it out a little ways from the alley's brick wall. Dana squatted down and peeked into the crack. A dirty white kitten with black spots mewed as it stared back at her.

Find the answers to these questions.

Who/What?: _____

Did What?: _____

When?: _____

Where?:_____

Why?: _____she wanted to find out what was making the crying noise_

What is the main idea?

ⓐ Dana finds a kitten behind a Dumpster and keeps it as her pet.

ⓑ Dana decides to hide her kitten behind a Dumpster in an alley.

ⓒ When Dana looks for the source of a noise, she finds a kitten.

Passage 7

As Polly and Suzie walked up the sidewalk to Mr. Zingo's run-down old house, a black cat streaked across their path. They looked at each other, but kept on moving. When they reached the porch, the front steps creaked loudly, as if to announce their arrival. Suzie looked around for a doorbell. Seeing none, she knocked on the door.

Mr. Zingo came to the door. "What do you want? I'm not buying whatever you're selling!" he said in a gruff tone.

Polly took a deep breath and replied, "We don't want to sell you anything. But we do want to ask you a favor."

"A favor, huh? What do you want?" Mr. Zingo practically snarled.

Suzie stood up as straight as she could and said, "We'd like to know if you would let us use that old treehouse in your woods. It looks like you don't use it anymore."

Find the answers to these questions.

Who/What?: _____

Did What?: _____

When?: _____

Where?: _____ at Mr. Zingo's front door _____

Why?: _____

What is the main idea?

ⓐ Mr. Zingo offers his old treehouse to Polly and Suzie.

ⓑ Polly and Suzie are terrified of Mr. Zingo.

ⓒ Polly and Suzie ask Mr. Zingo if they can use his old treehouse.

Picture a flag flying at the top of a flag pole. What do you notice first? The flag! The flag is like the main idea.

The flag pole holds up the flag. The flag pole is like the details. They hold up, or support, the main idea by:

☞   **telling more facts**

☞   **providing reasons**

☞   **giving examples**

Passage 1

Redwood trees are one of the longest-living plants on Earth. Many have already lived more than 2,000 years. Almost nothing can kill them. They do not die from disease. Bugs and fungi do not kill them. During a forest fire, the tree's bark may burn, but it will still survive. The same happens with lightning strikes. Over many years, the tree will slowly re-grow the bark and heal the scars. Those trees blown down by strong winds send up shoots from their roots. After a redwood tree is cut down, its stump will send up shoots.

What is the main idea?

ⓐ Redwood trees live longer than any other plant or animal on Earth.

ⓑ Redwood trees do not die easily.

ⓒ After a redwood tree is cut down, its stump will send up shoots.

Name 5 details that support the main idea:

1. _____

2. _____

3. _____

4. _____

5. _____

Passage 2

Roni knew that she shouldn't have listened to Lily. Yet here she stood, close to the edge of a small waterfall, looking down nervously into the crystal clear water below. Lily lounged on a warm, flat rock near the base of the falls, basking in the sun. She had already jumped off twice.

If Roni didn't jump, Lily would never let her live it down. Roni felt butterflies in her stomach. Why did she have to have such a daring younger sister? She couldn't leap; she felt too afraid. She looked around for a reasonable excuse to refuse to jump.

Suddenly, Roni's foot slipped on the slick wet rocks. Her legs went out from under her. She tried to catch her balance but failed. She plunged into the basin, hitting the water hard.

What is the main idea?

ⓐ Although Roni doesn't want to jump, she slips and falls into the water.

ⓑ Lily taunts her sister Roni and teases her when she won't jump into the water.

ⓒ Roni feels angry at Lily because she's so daring.

Name 6 details that support the main idea:

1. _____

2. _____

3. _____

4. _____

5. _____

6. _____

Passage 3

You know that you cannot drink salt water. If you do, you get more and more thirsty until you die. You must drink fresh water.

Can you guess how the Dead Sea got its name? The water in the Dead Sea is so salty that almost nothing can live in it. Its water has a higher salt content than the oceans! The extra salt in the water isn't all bad, though. It makes it easier for people to float. Many people enjoy swimming in the Dead Sea.

The Dead Sea lies between the nations of Israel and Jordan. This is a very dry area in the Middle East. The people use the Dead Sea water for drinking and growing crops. However, it must go through a special process to remove the salt. The process turns it into fresh water. It costs a lot of money. Yet in a place where there's little water, people have found a way to use what's available.

What is the main idea?

ⓐ People find it easy to float and swim in the salty Dead Sea.

ⓑ It is not healthy for people to drink salt water.

ⓒ Although the Dead Sea is salty, people have found a way to use its water.

Name 4 details that support the main idea:

1. _____

2. _____

3. _____

4. _____

Passage 4

Kyra straddled the tree limb. She felt thrilled and a little scared because she'd never climbed this high before. She could see all over her neighborhood. Rows of brown- and gray-shingled roofs stretched out in a grid. Next door, Mrs. Thatcher tended her tulip garden. Old Miss Travis snoozed in a lawn chair with an open book turned facedown on her lap. A dog sniffed around in a backyard. Farther away, a man with a bare chest pushed a lawn mower. From her perch in the tree, Kyra had a good view of everything.

What is the main idea?

ⓐ From her perch in the tree, Kyra had a good view of everything.

ⓑ Kyra had never before climbed so high in the tree.

ⓒ Kyra plays a trick on Mrs. Thatcher and Miss Travis.

Name 6 details that support the main idea:

1. _____

2. _____

3. _____

4. _____

5. _____

6. _____

Passage 5

Sponges and coral are animals that reproduce in an unusual way. They have their young by "budding." Their young start out as a growth on the outside of the parent's body. While it grows, the baby gets all of its food from the parent. When it is ready, it breaks away from the parent. Then it is a new, separate animal. From that moment on, it must take care of itself.

What is the main idea?

ⓐ While it grows, the baby sponge or coral gets all of its food from its parent.

ⓑ Sponges and coral reproduce in an unusual way.

ⓒ When it is ready, the young sponge or coral breaks away from its parent.

Name 4 details that support the main idea:

1. _____

2. _____

3. _____

4. _____

Passage 6

That evening the scouts gathered around the big screen TV in Andy's family room. Andy put a disc into the DVD player. He had just pushed the play button when Julio's cell phone rang. He immediately got up and left the room, covering one ear in order to hear more clearly. Within a minute, he came back into the room, his face pale and his eyes wide with fear.

"What's wrong, Julio? What's happened?" Andy asked.

"I think I was just threatened!" Julio said.

"What?" Andy cried. Everyone stared at Julio.

Julio was still so upset that his voice was little more than a whisper. "It was a man with a harsh voice. He said that if I don't stop trying to find the museum's missing key that I'd be sorry. Then he hung up."

What is the main idea?

ⓐ The scouts are enjoying an evening at the movies when Julio gets a call.

ⓑ Everyone stared at Julio.

ⓒ Julio gets threatened for trying to find the museum's missing key.

Name 3 details that support the main idea:

1. _____

2. _____

3. _____

Find the answers to these questions.

Who/What?: _____

Did What?: _____

When?: _____

Where?:_____

Why?: _____ a man wants to scare Julio from looking for a missing key

☞ **A topic sentence states the main idea.**

☞ **Nonfiction often has topic sentences.**

☞ **Topic sentences often come at the start of a passage and are followed by details.**

☞ **Topic sentences may fall in the middle of a passage. Then they have details before and after them.**

☞ **Sometimes topic sentences come at the end. They sum up the details that have come before.**

Passage 1

In Britain during the early 1800s, most peppered moths were gray with black spots. A few odd ones were black. The gray moths blended in with tree trunks. The black ones could easily be seen. So the birds ate them. They did not get to reproduce. The population of gray peppered moths stayed big. The population of black peppered moths stayed tiny.

Then in the mid 1800s, people built many factories. The smokestacks sent ashes into the air. This made the bark darken on the trees where the moths lived. Now the gray moths no longer blended in with the tree trunks. As a result, the birds ate them. They did not get to reproduce. More black peppered moths survived. Now most peppered moths in Britain are black. The species changed because of what humans did to their environment.

What is the topic sentence of this passage?

ⓐ Then in the mid 1800s, people built many factories.

ⓑ In Britain during the early 1800s, most peppered moths were gray with black spots

ⓒ The species changed because of what humans did to their environment.

Check one of the boxes to complete this sentence: The topic sentence comes at the ❑ beginning ❑ middle ❑ end of the passage.

What is the main idea?

ⓐ The population of black peppered moths stayed tiny.

ⓑ Humans can do things that cause species to change.

ⓒ People built many factories in Britain during the mid 1800s.

Passage 2

Tim put on his new hiking boots his parents had just bought for him. The boots had deep tread. Today, Tim planned to climb the Giant, the biggest rock in the state park. It was so large that all of the boulders around it looked puny. Every time his family had visited the park, he'd wanted to climb to the top of the Giant. Each time Tim had tried to climb the Giant, something went wrong. The first time it was just too steep. The next time he got scared halfway to the top. The last time his feet slipped and he couldn't get any footholds. His dad and older sister had already done it. Well, this time he would, too!

What is the topic sentence of this passage?

ⓐ Today, Tim planned to climb the Giant, the biggest rock in the state park.

ⓑ The Giant was so large that all of the boulders around it looked puny.

ⓒ Each time Tim had tried to climb the Giant, something went wrong.

Check one of the boxes to complete this sentence: The topic sentence comes at the ❑ beginning ❑ middle ❑ end of the passage.

What is the main idea?

ⓐ Tim admires his new hiking boots.

ⓑ Tim hopes to climb the Giant because he's always wanted to.

ⓒ Tim is jealous that his dad and older sister have already climbed the Giant.

Find the answers to these questions.

Who/What?: _____

Did What?: _____

When?: _____today_____

Where?:_____

Why?: _____

Passage 3

Rocks are always changing. They change slowly but constantly. On the Earth's surface they erode, or slowly wear away. Rain, ice, wind, and moving water break off little pieces. Sometimes these little pieces of rock get blown away. In other places, water carries them away. After the pieces drop, they form a new layer on the Earth's crust. Over time, more and more rock pieces cover them. In this way, a multitude of layers builds up.

After a very long time, heat and pressure squeeze the lowest layer. This makes the rocks get hotter and hotter. They begin to change. Rocks way down inside of the Earth get so hot that they melt. They become molten rock. Later they return to the Earth's crust as lava.

What is the topic sentence of this passage?

ⓐ On the Earth's surface rocks erode, or slowly wear away.

ⓑ Rocks are always changing.

ⓒ Rocks way down inside of the Earth get so hot that they melt.

Check one of the boxes to complete this sentence: The topic sentence comes at the ❏ beginning ❏ middle ❏ end of the passage.

What is the main idea?

ⓐ Whether on the surface or under the ground, rocks constantly change.

ⓑ Once rocks become molten, they only return to the surface as lava.

ⓒ Rocks change rapidly.

Passage 4

In late 1815 a volcano on an island in the South Pacific Ocean erupted. The force was equal to millions of atom bombs. It killed many people in the area. It caused trouble for people on the other side of the world, too. In 1816 the northeastern part of the U.S. and Canada had a "year without a summer." The summer months came just like always, but the weather was strange. It never got warm. It snowed in June. Every month had a killing frost. Although farmers planted crops, they died. The frost stopped the plants from growing.

At the time no one knew for sure what was happening. Now we know that the volcano threw dust and ash high into the sky. There was so much ash in the air that it blocked the sunlight. The sun's rays could not get through the layer of dirt. This kept North America colder than usual. It took a whole year for most of the ash to fall to the ground. Then temperatures went back to normal.

What is the topic sentence of this passage?

ⓐ It took a whole year for most of the ash to fall to the ground.

ⓑ In 1816 the northeastern part of the U.S. and Canada had a "year without a summer."

ⓒ The force was equal to millions of atom bombs.

Check one of the boxes to complete this sentence: The topic sentence comes at the ❑ beginning ❑ middle ❑ end of the passage.

What is the main idea?

ⓐ During the summer of 1816, nobody knew what caused the strange weather.

ⓑ In 1815 a volcano exploded, killing many people in the northeastern U.S. and Canada.

ⓒ A volcanic eruption caused an odd summer on the other side of the world.

Passage 5

Although Georgie the giraffe was just a baby, he was taller than any of the adults in his herd. In fact, he was the only one who could reach to the very top of the tallest tree in the area. Georgie felt so proud of himself that he bragged and showed off for the other giraffes whenever he got the chance.

One day, the herd of giraffes wandered to a new area. They came to a huge tree, taller than any other they had ever seen. Georgie wanted to show off. So he said, "Look at me! I can eat the leaves from the very top of this tall tree." With that he poked his head high up into the limbs of the gigantic tree. With a loud crack, several branches broke. They fell around his head, pinning down his ears. Georgie struggled, but the branches held him firmly. He cried to the rest of the giraffes, "Help me! My head is caught in the branches. I can't get loose!"

What is the topic sentence of this passage?

ⓐ Although Georgie the giraffe was just a baby, he was taller than any of the adults in his herd.

ⓑ The giraffes came to a huge tree, taller than any other they had ever seen.

ⓒ Georgie felt so proud of himself that he bragged and showed off for the other giraffes whenever he got the chance.

Check one of the boxes to complete this sentence: The topic sentence comes at the ❑ beginning ❑ middle ❑ end of the passage.

What is the main idea?

ⓐ The giraffe herd wanders around looking for the tallest trees to eat.

ⓑ Georgie Giraffe is so busy trying to show off that he ends up stuck in a tree.

ⓒ The other giraffes are deliberately mean to Georgie Giraffe.

Passage 6

My stomach rumbled with hunger. I continued walking, keeping a sharp eye out for berries. How come in books people always found berries to eat when they were lost? So far I had only seen a few berries. Since I didn't recognize them, I hadn't dared to eat them. If I didn't find some food soon, I might not have the strength to keep going.

The trail seemed to grow narrower. This wasn't a good sign. Perhaps I had gotten off the trail. I hadn't seen any yellow trail markers in at least an hour. I squinted up through the trees. Clouds had rolled in, completely blocking out the sun. I doubted I could have determined my position by it, but at least I might have a better idea of how long until the sunset. I felt like I was running out of time to find my way out of the woods before dark.

What is the topic sentence of this passage?

ⓐ I continued walking, keeping a sharp eye out for berries.

ⓑ I felt like I was running out of time to find my way out of the woods before dark.

ⓒ I hadn't seen any yellow trail markers in at least an hour.

Check one of the boxes to complete this sentence: The topic sentence comes at the ❑ beginning ❑ middle ❑ end of the passage.

What is the main idea?

ⓐ The writer is lost in the woods and afraid it will get dark soon.

ⓑ The writer is hungry but can't find any berries to eat.

ⓒ The writer is cold, lost, and hungry.

Passage 7

Long ago, when you needed new shoes, a cobbler made a pair just for you. You went to the cobbler's shop. He measured your feet. Then he chose the wooden or iron shoe form that matched your feet most closely. This shoe form was called a last. The cobbler used the last to make a leather upper. He also used the last to cut the one-inch thick soles the right size. Next, he sewed together the pieces of the upper. In the final step, he used tiny wooden pegs to attach the upper to the soles. All of this took several days.

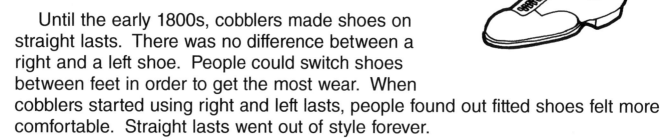

Until the early 1800s, cobblers made shoes on straight lasts. There was no difference between a right and a left shoe. People could switch shoes between feet in order to get the most wear. When cobblers started using right and left lasts, people found out fitted shoes felt more comfortable. Straight lasts went out of style forever.

What is the topic sentence of this passage?

ⓐ Straight lasts went out of style forever.

ⓑ Long ago, when you needed new shoes, a cobbler made a pair just for you.

ⓒ Until the early 1800s, cobblers made shoes on straight lasts.

Check one of the boxes to complete this sentence: The topic sentence comes at the ❑ beginning ❑ middle ❑ end of the passage.

What is the main idea?

ⓐ People's shoes used to be made by hand by a cobbler.

ⓑ People never liked shoes made on straight lasts.

ⓒ A cobbler could make a pair of shoes in a day.

Passage 8

A myth is a very old story that people once believed was true. Greek myths started around 5,000 years ago. Myths explained something—such as thunder—that people didn't understand. The Greeks thought that all natural things had spirits. They believed that clouds, land, plants, and water had feelings and could speak. Their myths had gods who had special powers. Many of their stories are still well known. We call them classic Greek mythology.

One well-known Greek myth explains why we hear an echo. Zeus, the highest god, told Echo to occupy his wife, Hera. He told her to talk a lot. This way Hera couldn't keep track of Zeus. Hera figured out his plan. She got mad at Echo. She took away Echo's voice. Poor Echo could only repeat the final word of anything she heard. Echo was in love with Narcissus. She followed him around. He ignored her. With her heart broken, she hid in a cave. She wasted away until only her voice remained.

What is the topic sentence of this passage?

ⓐ A myth is a very old story that people once believed was true.

ⓑ The Greeks thought that all natural things had spirits.

ⓒ Echo wasted away until only her voice remained.

Check one of the boxes to complete this sentence: The topic sentence comes at the ❑ beginning ❑ middle ❑ end of the passage.

What is the main idea?

ⓐ A girl hidden in a cave causes any echoes we hear.

ⓑ People in Ancient Greece believed myths were true stories that explained the world.

ⓒ Today many people think that the Greek myths are true.

The main idea is not always stated. This is often true in fiction. When the main idea is not given, ask questions to put together the main idea.

Passage 1

Churning butter was hard work. Maria's arms began to ache. She felt like she'd never finish. Maria stood back and looked at the pale, lumpy clumps and wiped her brow. Through the open door, she caught a glimpse of Jake walking toward the house. When he entered, she flashed her happiest smile. If Jake thought her chores looked more enjoyable than his own, perhaps he'd want to churn the butter.

Find the answers to these questions.

Who/What?: _____

Did What?: __flashed her happiest smile_____

When?: _____

Where?:_____

Why?: _____

What is the main idea?

ⓐ Maria's arms ache from churning butter.

ⓑ Jakes enjoys his chores more than Maria likes hers.

ⓒ Maria hopes Jake will want to churn the butter.

Passage 2

No one knows who first put wheels on a board and then tried to balance on it as it rolled. We do know that in the early 1950s surfers in California made the first skateboard that started the sport. They hadn't meant to invent a new sport. They just wanted to practice balancing a board on land. Some surfers put four roller-skate wheels on the bottom of a board. They took turns riding down the sidewalk. They called it "sidewalk surfing."

Other surfers saw their skateboard and wanted one. The surfboard companies began making skateboards, too. By the mid 1960s, kids all over the U.S. wanted them. Now the sport has spread all over the world.

A skateboarder rides a board with four wheels. The person needs good balance to control the board. Most people ride skateboards for fun. Other people use them to get around town. Pro riders can win money in contests. Each one tries to do the most exciting stunt. They do spins, flips, and grinds. It takes them years of work to get that good.

Find the answers to these questions.

Who/What?: _____surfers_____

Did What?: _____

When?: _____

Where?:_____

Why?: _____

What is the main idea?

ⓐ The sport of skateboarding began with surfers.

ⓑ Pro skateboarders win money by doing tricks in contests.

ⓒ Skateboarding was originally called sidewalk surfing.

Passage 3

"Break the cage latch with your paws or your teeth," the monkey advised.

The lion tried and tried, but he just couldn't free the monkey. The latch wouldn't budge. Suddenly, the animals saw the plane's cargo hatch closing. The door slammed, leaving them trapped.

Now the lion was angry and hungry. He roared, "You tricked me!"

"I did not! I had no idea the door would close!" The monkey shouted over the roar of the engines. The plane shook from the noise.

"What's going on?" roared the lion.

"I don't know!" answered the monkey.

The plane started to move—slowly at first, then faster and faster. The front of the plane lifted into the air, making the lion fall against the monkey's cage with such force that the latch broke open. After a few moments, both animals could move around.

"Where is the food you promised me?" the lion demanded. "Show it to me, or I'll eat you."

"Look here," said the monkey, hopping over to a stack of large bags. "Eat all you like."

"You lured me here to eat dry cat food? I should eat you right now!" snarled the lion.

Find the answers to these questions.

Who/What?: _____

Did What?: _____

When?: _____ he discovers the food he was promised is dry cat food

Where?:_____

Why?: _____

What is the main idea?

ⓐ The lion is mad at the monkey for trapping him in a cage.

ⓑ The lion gets upset when the monkey offers him dry cat food.

ⓒ The lion has to work hard to free the monkey from his cage.

Passage 4

Even though she was still in the village, Faith knew that her mother didn't like her to get this far from her home without permission. Still she kept walking, calling Lucky's name. She fought a sense of panic. She had to stay calm if she hoped to find Lucky. But Faith was running out of places to look. Surely the dog couldn't have gotten any farther than this. Maybe he had taken off in a different direction. Maybe he was hiding somewhere closer to home. Maybe he had gotten trapped someplace she'd never think to look. There were just too many possibilities!

Find the answers to these questions.

Who/What?: _____

Did What?: _____

When?: _____

Where?: _____while searching for her dog Lucky_____

Why?: _____

What is the main idea?

Ⓐ Faith has wandered far from home in search of a lost dog.

Ⓑ Faith gets lost when she goes looking for her missing dog.

Ⓒ Faith's mother gets upset when the family dog runs away.

Passage 5

The girls' search for wildflowers took them deeper into the woods than they'd ever gone before.

"Hey, Lynn, look over there," Molly said. "It looks like an old cabin. I never knew that anyone once lived in these woods. Let's explore it!"

Lynn looked doubtful. "What if somebody's living there? What if the floorboards are rotten and we fall through?"

"Oh don't be such a worrywart!" Molly exclaimed. "It'll be fun. There might be some old furniture left inside. Maybe we could use it as a clubhouse."

The girls approached the cabin. It looked as if it hadn't been lived in for a very long time. Cracked and peeling paint clung to the door and window frames. Several roof shingles had fallen, revealing the wood beneath. The windows had no panes left, and broken glass lay on the ground. Weeds pressed so close that the cabin seemed trapped.

"I don't like the looks of this place," Lynn protested. "Besides, I've got to go home and do some homework."

"How can you possibly have homework? School doesn't start again for another two weeks! Stop making up excuses and come on," Molly urged. She grabbed Lynn's hand and pulled her toward what was left of the front door.

Find the answers to these questions.

Who/What?: _____

Did What?: _____

When?: _____summer_____

Where?:_____

Why?: _____

What is the main idea?

ⓐ Lynn wants to do her homework but Molly won't let her.

ⓑ Molly wants the girls to turn the old cabin into a clubhouse.

ⓒ While looking for wildflowers, Molly and Lynn find an old cabin in the woods.

To select a title, first decide what the main idea is. Then check your choices to see which one best fits the topic.

Passage 1

Oil rigs are platforms in the sea. Beneath them is crude oil. A large drill goes down through the water, then through the rock. It keeps moving until it hits the oil. The drill is taken out, and a pipe replaces it. The oil flows up the pipe and gets collected. Tanker ships come to the oil rig and get the oil. Then they take it where it is needed.

In northern waters, planes search the waters every day to be sure that no floating icebergs will hit a rig. Sometimes, ships put a rope around the iceberg and tow it away from the rig. Other times, they may blow up the iceberg. As a last resort, the workers must pull up the oil pipe and unhook the platform's chains from posts driven into the ocean floor. Then they let the oil platform float out of the iceberg's way.

What is the main idea?

ⓐ Planes search northern waters in order to protect oil rigs.

ⓑ Oil rigs need to be kept safe from floating icebergs.

ⓒ Tanker ships carry oil from oil rigs to the places where it's needed.

What would be the best title for this passage?

ⓐ Icebergs Threaten Oil Rigs

ⓑ Oil Rigs and Tanker Ships

ⓒ Drilling for Oil at Sea

Passage 2

In 1986 tiny animals came to the Great Lakes. A few zebra mussels had clung to a big ship. The ship came from the sea. It brought the mussels into the lake. The animals there had never seen a zebra mussel. They did not eat them. This let the mussels multiply quickly. The little striped creatures spread from one lake to another. After a while, all of the Great Lakes had too many zebra mussels.

The zebra mussels have changed the environment in the Great Lakes. They eat algae. Removing algae makes water clearer and more acidic*. This may not sound bad, but it has caused problems. Some other animals have died off. In some cases, there wasn't enough algae left for them to eat. In other cases, the more acidic water was bad for them.

*greater amount of acid

zebra mussels

What is the main idea?

ⓐ Zebra mussels eat algae, causing water to become clearer.

ⓑ Zebra mussels have changed the Great Lakes' environment.

ⓒ In 1986 zebra mussels arrived in the Great Lakes.

What would be the best title for this passage?

ⓐ The Environment of the Great Lakes

ⓑ The Great Lakes' Newest Animal

ⓒ Zebra Mussels Cause Trouble in the Great Lakes

What is the topic sentence?

ⓐ The zebra mussels have changed the environment in the Great Lakes.

ⓑ The little striped creatures spread from one lake to another.

ⓒ In 1986 tiny animals came to the Great Lakes.

Check one of the boxes to complete this sentence: The topic sentence comes at the ❑ beginning ❑ middle ❑ end of the passage.

Passage 3

A tale says that Atlantis was once a continent. People lived there in beautiful cities. Then one day it sank to the bottom of the Atlantic Ocean. All this took place thousands of years ago.

Around 300 B.C. a man named Plato wrote about Atlantis. He wrote that big explosions occurred there. After that, the land disappeared.

For hundreds of years, people have looked for Atlantis. Some scientists think that they may have found it. They say that it is beneath the Agean Sea. About 3,500 years ago, an island was there. Then its volcano blew up. This made a huge hole in the island. Seawater rushed in. The land flooded, making it look as if it sank.

What is the main idea?

ⓐ Atlantis lies at the bottom of the Agean Sea.

ⓑ According to a tale, there is a missing continent called Atlantis.

ⓒ People started searching for Atlantis immediately after its disappearance.

What would be the best title for this passage?

ⓐ The Lost Continent

ⓑ Submarine Explores Atlantis

ⓒ Atlantis: Jewel of the Atlantic Ocean

What is the topic sentence?

ⓐ Since then people have looked for Atlantis.

ⓑ The land flooded, making it look as if it sank.

ⓒ A tale says that Atlantis was once a continent.

Check one of the boxes to complete this sentence: The topic sentence comes at the ❑ beginning ❑ middle ❑ end of the passage.

Passage 4

The platypus is an Australian mammal with webbed feet and a wide, flat tail. It lives near shallow streams. As it swims along, it uses its wide, flat snout to scoop up worms and shellfish from the stream bottoms. On land, its claws help it to walk and to dig.

Unlike most mammals, the platypus lays eggs. The female digs a burrow in the bank of a stream. She uses leaves and grass to build a nest at the far end of her burrow. Next, she completely blocks the burrow's opening with dirt. Then she lays two or three eggs. After ten days, the babies hatch. The babies stay with her, drinking her milk for four months.

What is the main idea?

ⓐ A platypus uses its wide, flat snout to scoop up worms and shellfish from the stream bottoms.

ⓑ Platypus babies are not like other mammals because they drink their mother's milk.

ⓒ The platypus is an unusual mammal that lives in Australia.

What would be the best title for this passage?

ⓐ An Odd Mammal

ⓑ Nests in Australia

ⓒ Animals that Lay Eggs

Passage 5

Toads catch bugs with their tongues. They swallow them whole. Baby toads are the same size as many bugs. Yet no adult toad ever mistakes a baby toad for an insect. Toads can see a glow on another toad's skin, so they don't eat each other.

During its first summer, a toad grows so fast that it sheds its skin every three days. It develops the bumps on its skin while it hibernates during its first winter. These bumps fill with fluid. Some people call it "toad poison." It's not real poison, but it can make your eyes sting if it gets in them. This fluid makes the toad taste bad to some animals. If they catch a toad, they spit it out unharmed.

Years ago, people believed that if you handled a toad, you'd get warts. They thought the "toad poison" made the warts form. Now we know that a germ causes warts. Warts have nothing to do with toads.

What is the main idea?

ⓐ Toads develop bumps on their skin while they hibernate during their first winter.

ⓑ A toad's skin has special features to keep it from being eaten by other toads or predators.

ⓒ A toad's skin has toad poison that will make your eyes sting if it gets in them.

What would be the best title for this passage?

ⓐ Poisonous Toads

ⓑ Toads to the Rescue

ⓒ Toads Have Special Skin

Passage 6

The cat teetered on the edge of the open box, then fell in. Before he could climb out, a worker closed the lid. Inside the dark box, the cat cried, "Meow-meow. I'm stuck! Meow-meow."

No one heard him. Soon, a truck carried his box to the launch site. Then the cat felt like he was going up on an elevator. His box jolted and moved. A door closed with a large bang. "Meow-meow. I'm scared. Meow-meow," the cat said.

Then came a huge roaring sound as the space shuttle took off. "Meow-meow! Help! Help! Meow-meow!" the cat cried as his box shook. After several minutes of terror, the cat felt like he was floating. He was enjoying the feeling when suddenly the box's top opened. "Meoww…" screeched the cat, floating up out of the box. He saw a startled astronaut, whose eyes were wide with surprise.

"What are you doing here?" she asked with a smile. "Come, look everyone! We have a stow-away!" Several crewmembers came over to see the floating cat.

What is the main idea?

ⓐ A cat jumps into a box so it can hitch a ride on the space shuttle.

ⓑ An astronaut finds her next pet when she discovers a cat on the space shuttle.

ⓒ A cat gets trapped inside a box and is later freed on the space shuttle.

What would be the best title for this passage?

ⓐ Space Shuttle Stowaway

ⓑ The Frightened Cat

ⓒ The First Animal in Space

Passage 7

In Britain, an odd monument stands in the midst of farm fields. Its name is Stonehenge. It is a set of giant stone slabs. These slabs are grouped in circles. Scientists believe that it is thousands of years old. No one knows who built Stonehenge or why. Some think it served as a calendar. Others think that people used the stones to watch the sky. They could track the movement of the sun, stars, and moon. Still others think that people held religious rites there.

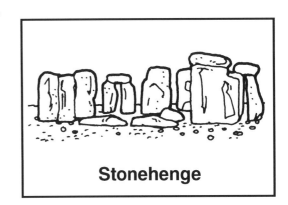

Stonehenge

Over time, the huge stones fell over. People took some away for other uses. The British government decided to restore Stonehenge in 1922. Workers found some of the missing stones. They put them back in their places. Now Stonehenge is one of the nation's most popular places to visit. Over one million people go there each year.

What is the main idea?

ⓐ People are fascinated by Stonehenge and wonder who built it and why.

ⓑ Workers found some of the missing stones when the British government decided to restore Stonehenge.

ⓒ Stonehenge, a set of giant stone slabs in Britain, was used as an ancient calendar.

What would be the best title for this passage?

ⓐ Giant Stone Slabs

ⓑ A Popular British Monument

ⓒ The Mysterious Place Called Stonehenge

What is the topic sentence?

ⓐ The British government decided to restore Stonehenge in 1922.

ⓑ In Britain, an odd monument stands in the midst of farm fields.

ⓒ Now Stonehenge is one of the nation's most popular places to visit.

Check one of the boxes to complete this sentence: The topic sentence comes at the ❑ beginning ❑ middle ❑ end of the passage.

Passage 1

The baby snapping turtle was too far from the river. Jody looked around for its nest. Maybe the mother turtle had laid its eggs far from shore. She saw no other turtles. Jody frowned. There was no way she could leave it on the bike path; it would surely get run over. It looked so small and helpless. What should she do?

Jody crossed her arms as she squatted above the turtle. She was scared of snapping turtles! Her parents had told her to avoid them. She knew she should walk away and leave it to die, but she just couldn't do that. Jody had to find a way to get the baby snapping turtle to the water where it would at least have a chance.

Jody didn't dare pick up the turtle, so she found two twigs. She used them to prod the baby snapper toward the riverbank about a dozen yards away. It took a few steps, then halted. It refused to budge. Now Jody felt certain that there was no way it had the strength to make it to the water on its own.

Jody slipped off one sneaker. As gently as she could, she used the twigs like a pair of chopsticks. She picked up the tiny turtle and set it inside of her shoe. Then she carefully made her way toward the river, eyes glued to the ground. It wouldn't be good to run into another snapper with no shoe on one foot!

What is the main idea?

ⓐ A mother turtle laid its eggs too far from the river.

ⓑ Jody is frightened when she comes across a snapping turtle on the bike path.

ⓒ Jody finds a baby snapping turtle and thinks of a way to get it to the river.

What is the topic sentence?

ⓐ Jody had to find a way to get the baby snapping turtle to the water where it would at least have a chance.

ⓑ It wouldn't be good to run into another snapper with no shoe on one foot!

ⓒ Jody didn't dare pick up the turtle, so she found two twigs.

What would be the best title for this passage?

ⓐ Fear on the Bike Path

ⓑ Snapping Turtle Rescue

ⓒ Jody Makes a Decision

Passage 2

Most plants have roots, leaves, and stems, each of which helps the plant to thrive. Roots hold the plant in the ground. Tiny hairs on the roots take in water and nutrients from the soil. Some roots store the food made by the plant.

The main job of a plant's leaves is to make food for the plant through the process of photosynthesis. Since they contain chlorophyll, leaves can use sunlight, water, and carbon dioxide to make their own food. Plants use this food to live and grow. A plant's leaves also let off water vapor from their undersides.

Most plants' stems hold their leaves up to the sunlight. The stem also serves as a passageway to the rest of the plant. The minerals and water taken in by the roots move through the stem to the leaves. Food made in the leaves travels in the stem to the plant's flowers and fruits or goes down the stem to be stored in the roots.

What is the main idea?

ⓐ Plants make food to live and grow.

ⓑ The roots, stems, and leaves of a plant all have important roles.

ⓒ The main job of a plant's leaves is to make food for the plant through the process of photosynthesis.

What is the topic sentence?

ⓐ Food made in the leaves travels in the stem to the plant's flowers and fruits or goes down the stem to be stored in the roots.

ⓑ Since they contain chlorophyll, leaves can use sunlight, water, and carbon dioxide to make their own food.

ⓒ Most plants have roots, leaves, and stems, each of which helps the plant to thrive.

What would be the best title for this passage?

ⓐ Plant Parts and Their Purposes

ⓑ Plants that Make Food

ⓒ Making Food from the Sun

Passage 3

Toward midday, the boys reached a spot where the road had been cut out of the hillside on the right. On their left, jagged wet rocks lay at the base of a steep cliff. Ocean waves crashed on the rocks. Mack looked over at his friend Bill.

"This road seems pretty narrow. There's almost no shoulder for us to ride on," he said.

"Don't worry. We'll be through this part soon," Bill responded calmly, shifting gears on his bike. Having lived in Clifton his whole life, he knew the area much better than Mack.

As the boys came to a sharp curve, Mack glanced back over his shoulder to see how far behind his younger brother was. Suddenly, a loud rumbling sound and a spray of dirt and rocks ripped through the air.

"Landslide!" Bill shouted. "Come on Mack! We've got to get out of here!"

But Mack had frozen. His brother was on the other side of the landslide. Could he stop his bike fast enough to avoid running into the pile of rocks?

What is the main idea?

ⓐ A sudden landslide separates bicyclists.

ⓑ Bill and Mack struggle to save a boy who's buried under a landslide.

ⓒ The narrow road makes bike riding dangerous for the boys.

What is the topic sentence?

ⓐ Toward midday, the boys reached a spot where the road had been cut out of the hillside on the right.

ⓑ Suddenly, a loud rumbling sound and a spray of dirt and rocks ripped through the air.

ⓒ Having lived in Clifton his whole life, Bill knew the area much better than Mack.

What would be the best title for this passage?

ⓐ The Exciting Bike Ride

ⓑ Over the Edge of the Cliff!

ⓒ Landslide!

Answer Key

Page 5

   1. c

   2. a

Page 6

   1. b

   2. c

Page 7

   1. c

   2. b

Page 8

   1. a

   2. b

Page 9

   1. a

   2. c

Page 10

   1. c

   2. b

Page 11

   1.

who/what: Eve

did what: tried to light a fire

when: at night

where: in the forest

why: because it was so dark

   2. b

Page 12

   1.

who/what: Amelia Earhart & Fred Noonan

did what: vanished

when: July 2, 1937

where: Pacific Ocean

why: no one knows

   2. a

Page 13

   1.

who: George

did what: got annoyed at Ralph

when: Ralph drags George to a garage sale

where: at a garage sale

why: Ralph only brought 10 cents to spend

   2. c

Page 14

   1.

who/what: Dan & Ron

did what: hid behind crates

when: they heard someone coming

where: inside a room

why: they don't want to be caught

Page 15

   1.

who/what: Joe Terry

did what: rescued two little children

when: August 1995

where: railroad tracks in CA

why: because the train would've killed them

   2. b

Page 16

   1.

who/what: Dana

did what: finds a dirty white kitten

when: after she hears a noise in the alley

where: behind a dumpster in the alley

why: she wanted to find out what was making the noise

   2. c

Page 17

   1.

who/what: Polly and Suzie

did what: ask Mr. Zingo's permission

when: after Mr. Zingo's opens the door

where: at his front door

why: they want to use his old tree-house

   2. c

Page 18

   1. *b*

   2. *details*: don't die from disease; not killed by bugs or fungi; bark re-grows after forest fire or lightning strike; when blown down, send up new shoots; when cut down, send up new shoots

Page 19

   1. *a*

   2. *details*: Roni had butterflies in her stomach; she felt too afraid to leap; she looked around for an excuse not to jump; her foot slipped on wet rocks; her legs went out from under her; she fell into the water

Page 20

   1. *c*

   2. *details*: Dead Sea water is so salty nothing can live in it; higher salt content than the oceans; people need Dead Sea water; it goes through a special, costly process to get rid of the salt

Page 21

   1. *a*

   2. *details*: she could see all over her neighborhood; rows of roofs stretched out in a grid; Mrs. Thatcher tended her tulip garden; Miss Travis slept in a lawn chair; a dog sniffs around a yard; man pushing lawn mower

Page 22

   1. *b*

   2. *details*: have young by budding; babies start as growth on parent's body; baby gets food from parent; eventually breaks away and must take care of itself

Page 23

   1. c

   2. *details*: Julio gets a phone call; Julio is so upset that his voice was little more than a whisper; a man told Julio he'd be sorry if he kept trying to find the museum's key

   3.

who/what: Julio

did what: got a threatening phone call

when: evening

where: Andy's family room

why: a man wants to scare him away from looking for the museum key

Answer Key

Page 24
1. c
2. end
3. b

Page 25
1. a
2. beginning
3. b
4.
who/what: Tim
did what: plans to climb the Giant
when: today
where: at the state park
why: he's always wanted to climb it

Page 26
1. b
2. beginning
3. a

Page 27
1. b
2. middle
3. c

Page 28
1. c
2. middle
3. b

Page 29
1. b
2. end
3. a

Page 30
1. b
2. beginning
3. a

Page 31
1. a
2. beginning
3. b

Page 32
1.
who/what: Maria
did what: flashed her happiest smile
when: Jake enters the house
where: inside the house

why: she wants him to take over churning butter
2. c

Page 33
1.
who/what: surfers
did what: started the sport of skateboarding
when: early 1950s
where: in California
why: so they could practice their balance on land
2. a

Page 34
1.
who/what: the lion
did what: gets upset
when: he discovers the food he was promised is dry cat food
where: in the plane's cargo hold
why: he expected better food
2. b

Page 35
1.
who/what: Faith
did what: wanders far from home
when: while searching for her dog Lucky
where: far from home
why: the dog is missing
2. a

Page 36
1.
who/what: Molly and Lynn
did what: find an old abandoned cabin
when: summer
where: deep in the woods
why: they're out looking for wild-flowers
2. c

Page 37
1. b
2. a

Page 38
1. b
2. c
3. a
4. middle

Page 39
1. b
2. a
3. c
4. beginning

Page 40
1. c
2. a

Page 41
1. b
2. c

Page 42
1. c
2. a

Page 43
1. a
2. c
3. b
4. beginning

Page 44
1. c
2. a
3. b

Page 45
1. b
2. c
3. a

Page 46
1. a
2. b
3. c

Made in the USA
Las Vegas, NV
21 August 2021